Diary of an Everyday Millionaire: My Secrets to Building a Real Estate Empire

Kevin McNeely, MBA

This publication is designed to provide accurate and authoritative information in regard to the subject matter covered. It is sold with the understanding that the publisher or author is not engaged in rendering legal, accounting, or other professional service. If legal advice or other expert assistance is required, the services of a competent professional person should be sought.

Editor: Kevin McNeely

Cover Design: Kevin McNeely

Typesetting: Kevin McNeely

*D*edication

This book is dedicated to my children - Summer and Christian and all the other aspiring millionaires of the future. May your hard work, dedication and willingness to take a risk get you to your goals.

*I*ntroduction

It's tangible, it's solid, it's beautiful. It's artistic, from my standpoint, and I just love real estate.

- Donald Trump

The most effective learning comes from experience. Over the years, I've made a lot of real estate deals. Some resulted in profitable outcomes; some were not-so-profitable. However, each transaction was a valuable learning experience. I'm very close to millionaire status so further profit is not my chief motivation for writing this book. Money is no longer an issue for me. The main reason, I'm writing this book is to capture my experiences for my children. I'm hopeful they will avoid many of the mistakes I made in the past when it comes to evaluating, buying, trading and holding real estate.

I hope this book stimulates critical thinking. As you read through my experiences, I encourage you to question my thoughts, guidance and opinions. Ask yourself, why did he do that? Why does he say that? I fully encourage and respect your right to disagree. In the end, we may agree to disagree.

Questioning and disagreement is the root of critical thinking. Words on parchment are just words. Every individual has the duty to independently research and dissect each concept I suggest. My concepts, thoughts and opinions are possibly just one step away from a revolutionary, new approach. You may have this step stored somewhere in your mind. Perhaps a single keyword or phrase I mention in this book will unleash it.

This book is meant for beginning real estate investors but I hope more seasoned, veterans of the real estate business will find a nugget or two. It is meant to provide foundational information about finding, buying and holding real estate. Advanced topics are intentionally avoided but I will likely explore those topics in future publications.

I have tried to avoid technical language wherever possible. All too often, men and women with advanced degrees attempt to demonstrate their intelligence by using big words and complex phrases. All too often, these same "big brains" totally miss connecting with their audience. Their message is lost in a jungle of large words and technical jargon. Ultimately, their "big brains" are not big enough because they fail to consider the chief purpose of their written communication.

Their purpose is to pass information in a manner that is simple, understandable and easily understood. For those of you who read my first book, **"Get Rich Off A Minimum Wage Income"**, you will see familiar concepts again. This is required because the information is inter-connected. The truth is these key concepts deserve reinforcing because they are so vital to your success.

This is not really a guide for buying your primary residence. It is written for the beginning real estate investor. It is written with the idea of profiting off real estate in the short, intermediate and long term. It is written with idea the reader is seeking serious wealth accumulation. If you are looking to just purchase your primary home, pursue other books dedicated to that purpose. However, if you hope to own more than one property at some point, this book is for you.

So what makes me qualified to write a book on real estate? I'll be the first to tell you my Master's of Business Administration degree **does not** qualify me to write this book. The world is full of highly educated people who barely get by. It is also full of highly educated people with book smarts but no street smarts. You need intelligence and **intuition** to win in life. No book in the world can teach intuition. There is no book in the world that fully teaches you to sniff out a good real estate deal. What about guts? Is there a book out there somewhere that teaches you to accept risk? Is there a book to teach you to go for it? No. You must find these qualities within you.

What makes me qualified to write a book? I have almost a million dollars in cash and assets. I am nearly the millionaire living next door. I have set myself up to retire completely at 42 years old and not work a day for the rest of my life. That and that alone is why I am qualified to write this book. Now, I will pass a lifetime of experiences over to you.

Chapter 1

In the real estate business you learn more about people, and you learn more about community issues, you learn more about life, you learn more about the impact of government, probably more than any other profession that I know of.

- Johnny Isakson

Why buy real estate?

I have accumulated most of my wealth in the stock market. In fact, I have made a small fortune in financial markets. The gist of my wealth is still in the stock market today. It is an undisputed fact that over time, stocks outperform real estate. Using data provided by National Association of Realtors and the New York University School of Business, let us study historical rate of return from real estate vs. historical returns from the S&P 500 over a 36-year period.

Real Estate	% Increase	S&P 500	% Increase
1969	6.00%	1969	-8.24%
1970	8.00%	1970	3.56%
1971	7.80%	1971	14.22%
1972	7.70%	1972	18.76%
1973	8.20%	1973	-14.31%
1974	10.70%	1974	-25.90%
1975	10.30%	1975	37.00%
1976	7.90%	1976	23.83%

1977	12.50%	1977	-6.98%
1978	13.50%	1978	6.51%
1979	14.20%	1979	18.52%
1980	11.90%	1980	31.74%
1981	6.80%	1981	-4.70%
1982	2.10%	1982	20.42%
1983	3.70%	1983	22.34%
1984	3.00%	1984	6.15%
1985	4.30%	1985	31.24%
1986	6.40%	1986	18.49%
1987	6.60%	1987	5.81%
1988	4.10%	1988	16.54%
1989	0.20%	1989	31.48%
1990	2.80%	1990	-3.06%
1991	5.50%	1991	30.23%
1992	2.70%	1992	7.49%
1993	3.40%	1993	9.97%
1994	4.00%	1994	1.33%
1995	3.10%	1995	37.20%
1996	4.80%	1996	22.68%
1997	5.20%	1997	33.10%
1998	5.40%	1998	28.34%
1999	3.80%	1999	20.89%
2000	4.30%	2000	-9.03%
2001	6.30%	2001	-11.85%
2002	5.70%	2002	-21.97%
2003	8.50%	2003	28.36%
2004	9.30%	2004	10.74%
Average	**6.41%**	**Average**	**11.97%**

In this case study, stocks are the clear winner. Do you recall I asked you to question anything and everything? This data sparks an interesting question, why invest in real estate at all?

Look at the data again, using a 36-year sample of actual-factual, financial data. The S&P annual average is 11.97% while the annual average for real estate is 6.41%. I will ask you again, why invest in real estate at all? I have asked myself this same question. In fact, I have spent many lonely nights in my home office buried in financial reports, figures and information searching for the answers. After years of experience and countless hours of deep thought, I have concluded there are three reasons you should invest in real estate despite the undisputed fact stocks will outperform real estate over time.

Reason #1: The Incredible Power of Leverage

First, you have to understand what leverage is. According to my favorite website Investopedia.com, leverage is "The use of various financial instruments or borrowed capital, such as margin, to increase the potential return of an investment." Let me explain what this means in simple terms. Leverage is simply debt. It is similar to debt you carry on your credit card but with a slight difference. Leverage is debt that makes money for you. That is the critical distinction. Credit card debt takes money from you. Leverage results in a net gain when all the expenses are paid.

Can you use the power of leverage in stocks? Sure, you can. It is called investing on the **margin** but it is not nearly as powerful as real estate leverage. The first weakness of investing on the margin is it carries considerable risk. In fact, there is a deadly phenomenon called a **margin call** that will surely ruin your day.

Another weakness of using leverage with stocks is interest rates. Stocks are very volatile vehicles; lenders recognize this credit risk so they impose a higher interest rate on margin accounts. Let me give you an example. I will pull current annual percentage rates for a multi-family property from Bell County in Texas. This is place where I hold the majority of my real estate holdings. Using current interest rates pulled from Bankrate.com on November 30th, 2013 - the most competitive annual percentage rate I found was 4.162%. Now let us compare it with a competitive margin account from a leading investment brokerage firm, the same kind of accounts used to borrow money to invest in the stock market. The current rate is 6% for a $200,000 loan. The margin interest rate called the "**margin interest schedule**" is computed using the base lending rate plus the interest rate. The rates vary depending on the amount of money an investor wants to borrow; the larger the loan, the lower the interest rate and smaller the loan, the higher the interest rate.

Using the example above, **the cost of borrowing is 1.838% higher** with regards to stocks. In the quest for riches, every percentage point counts.

Leverage is the process of creating instant wealth out of thin air and if the real estate is wisely chosen, it is permanent in its value.

Leverage is not risk-free. It is important you understand that. Leverage will demand monthly payments at regularly scheduled intervals. In the business world, this is often referred to as **servicing your debt**. Whether you use real estate leverage or stock leverage, you have to make your payments. In margin investing, financial institutions will likely seize other liquid assets if you don't repay your loan. In the world of real estate, your real estate empire will undergo **foreclosure**.

These unfortunate events will be major setbacks for you so using leverage must be done wisely. Careful thought, planning and consideration must happen prior to closing the deal. In the case of real estate investing, a house you cannot rent on the market isn't worth the cost of a roll of used toilet paper.

Before you embark on your first deal using leverage, spend a lot of time talking with those familiar with its use. Discuss the potential possibilities and using their wisdom, analyze the possible risks.

Reason #2: Current Income

We all want money in our pocket. Every day, millions of Americans report to work to earn money. If I had to guess, I'd say you are reading this book today in order to learn about new ways of making money. Here is a tip for you. Real estate and, in most cases, stocks will both generate money for you. But stocks will not generate as much money for you. There is a certain category of stocks called growth stocks that will not pay you any money whatsoever. Therefore, if you are using stocks as an investment vehicle to generate current income, it is important you understand that. Since real estate and stocks, in most cases, create income. Which one creates more?

Using another example to answer this question, let us pretend we have $100,000 to invest. We will invest $50,000 in a stock mutual fund and $50,000 we will use as a down payment to purchase a multi-family apartment building. Which one do you think will generate more income on a monthly basis?

Without accepting incredible risk, your best mutual funds will return an **SEC yield** of about 2% annually. The SEC yield is probably one of the best methods for determining how much money a mutual fund will payout annually. I will try to explain SEC yields in simple terms. Over the course of any given year, mutual fund brokerage firms receive income from the individual stocks in their holdings. For example, Pepsi sells soft drinks. The corporation receives money for each soft drink sold. The corporation keeps most of the money but it will give a small amount of money to the individual shareholders as a gesture of goodwill. Mutual funds hold stocks on behalf of the fund holders so the fund will collectively receive these small amounts of money. When it is all said and done, this small amount is actually a large sum. The mutual fund will take this money and its operating costs which may include paying accountants, customer service representatives, fund managers, business analysts and the list goes on and on. After all expenses are paid, the mutual fund holders (that's you) get what is left. This is your dividend yield. Using our example, your dividend yield on $50,000 is $1,000. Even though, it is just $1,000, always keep things in perspective. That is one month's pay for some people and you just earned that by sitting on your behind for one year. Let us look at our income from a stock fund monthly. This will be important later on. With this example, we earn a whopping **$83.33** a month.

What happens if we put $50,000 in real estate? The result varies depending on what part of the country you live. The price of real estate varies upon geographical location. For this example, we will use real estate prices in Texas simply because I love the state so much. There are no state income taxes so you should consider loving it too! The rest of this scenario is built using an actual property in the city of Killeen listed on the Multiple Listing Service (MLS) from November 30, 2013.

Fifty thousand dollars in the great state of Texas, qualifies for a $200,000 real estate loan assuming 25% is the required down payment. Residential properties normally only require 20% down but lenders consider multi-family dwellings riskier. Hence, they require a higher down payment. Despite, the higher upfront costs, you can find a fourplex, multi-family building for that amount of money. The MLS normally lists rent-per-unit amounts. I am looking for that data now. Okay, I found it. On this example, the units are renting for $780 each and every unit is occupied. Finding a property with all units occupied is fantastic. It immediately takes a degree of stress off you since one of your greatest challenges as a land owner is keeping your units occupied and rented with good tenants. Let us do the math and see what we come up with. Our monthly cash flow from this single building is **$3,120**. Now most people will have expenses so this is not a true figure. You will likely spend a portion on repairs. Perhaps, you may have to pay money to replace a faulty ceiling fan. You will spend money on property taxes and property insurance. Perhaps, you will have to pay money for a management firm to oversee rent collection and evictions among other duties. What about advertising costs? People will move so you will have to get the word out to get new tenants. You will definitely pay about a third of that money to service your debt. By now, I think you understand. You will have expenses but you will have to spend a lot of money to end up with just $83.33. Here is the advantage real estate has over stock mutual funds. **Real estate normally generates more income now.**

A lot of people are lured to real estate for that fact. Can you blame them? Our bills run on a monthly cycle. Once a month, you pay utilities, cable, cell phone, internet and your mortgage. Guess what? Real estate pays monthly too. Most stock mutual funds pay out either quarterly or annually. Many people do not like that fact. I know I don't.

Reason #3: Diversification

There is one more reason you should invest in real estate despite the fact stocks kicks real estate butt in long-term performance. The final reason is diversification. Return to the chart above and reference the year 1974. In that year, stocks returned a dismal -25.90%. In that very same year, real estate returned 10.70%. That is the very reason you should have real estate as part of your portfolio of assets.

Now, I am sure someone is out there is thinking; *Well, if that person didn't sell their stocks, they still would have kicked real estate's butt in the long run.* That is a good point and it is totally true but the majority of people do not have that kind of discipline to hold stocks in a down market. We, as people, have a natural tendency to want to sell when we are faced with probable lost. We think the following thoughts. *We have a mortgage to pay! We have a family to feed! What if, the market goes to zero! This could be the end-of-days, I read about in the Bible!*

The truth is most people will sell in a down market and ruin their portfolio. Some will ruin their lives. Fortunes are made and lost in the market every day. A portion of your portfolio dedicated to real estate will help you bring some order to the disorder. Real estate is simply less volatile than stocks over the long haul. Real estate will help you stay the course.

I have presented you with three compelling reasons to include well thought out real estate holding as part of your portfolio. You need to find the right mixture of stocks, bonds and real estate that works for you. At the time of this writing, 42% of my holdings are in real estate. This is a bit high for me but I found the opportunity of a lifetime and I went for it. I acquired another fantastic single-family home at the right price, in the right neighborhood. It was a deal I couldn't pass up.

There is one thing I have learned about opportunity. At one moment, it is here. At another moment, it is gone. Those who hesitate are simply left behind – tortured by a lifetime of regrets.

Chapter 2

Now, one thing I tell everyone is learn about real estate. Repeat after me: real estate provides the highest returns, the greatest value and the least risk.

- Armstrong Williams

How do I find great real estate deals?

So you have decided real estate is for you. Good for you! Now, the hard part is finding good deals. I wish I had some secret I could share with you that will guarantee returns but I don't. Finding the best deals is a mixture of science and art. Sure, I will show you where to find properties. Sure, I will show you some techniques to determine value. Sure, I will give you tactics, techniques and procedures I use to determine a good deal. Yet, ultimately, it will come down to your gut because no one can predict the future.

After all the data is analyzed, after your realtors give their predictions, after the surveys and the appraisals, you will have to stare at that property and make your call. That is why I never purchase a property strictly off the internet. I know this is a growing trend but it is one I will never, ever subscribe to. I need to see it with my own eyes. I need to feel the pulse of the neighborhood. I need to see the residents in action – going about their daily lives. After all the data is analyzed, I rely on my guts to make the final call. Some people call it instincts while others call it intuition. Whatever you call it – it is your deciding factor and it should outweigh all other data.

Without instincts and guts to go for it, you will be paralyzed by fear and you will secure your place in mediocrity.

Okay, you have that. Now you are ready to find some deals. How do you do it? Where do you go? In the olden days, we drive endlessly around cities and neighbors, constantly vigilant for homes on the market. Each red and white "For Sale" sign spoke of fruitful profits and endless possibilities.

In the past, we would scour our local newspaper looking for possible deals that could result in positive outcomes. In days long gone, we would sit at county courthouse steps, waiting like vultures for the next property auction to begin. Those days are long gone and they are not coming back.

Today we use the internet. We are able to surf the web in search of our golden egg from the comfort of our home. I often look for deals in my pajamas. Sometimes, I sip a glass of wine and surf the web. Whenever, I have a free moment, I am searching across the entire country looking for acquisitions, at the right price.

In contemporary times, information is money! The person who gets the information the fastest will always emerge the victor. I cannot speak to what the country or the internet will look like 10 years from now but I can tell you what information sources I use today.

My main source for finding great deals is **Zillow.com**. Zillow is real estate information marketplace that connects buyers to sellers and borrowers to lenders. Its offers estimated home values, rental price estimates and property tax information. A world of information is available for your own analysis on this website alone. Using Zillow, you can track estimated property values. You may have good deal if you find a property significantly priced lower than its estimate.

Before you rush out and it buy though, you need to consider other factors. Is the structure physically sound? In other words, the foundation must be good and stable. If you purchase a property and it has structural problems, this is costly expense. Foundation problems can costs in excess of $10,000. What about the neighborhood? Is it declining? Do street gangs control the block? These factors will affect your bottom-line. A good deal is priced well-below market value, in a decent neighborhood and only requires cosmetic, low-cost repairs. Over time, through experience, you will learn to smell a good deal if you do this long enough. I shoot for properties priced 20% below market values. I have known friends who have secured a good property for 25% below. Although, I have had no such luck I know those deals exist and if you stumble upon one, hastily but thoroughly conduct your analysis and go for!

I use another website to hunt down deals. It is called **Realtor.com**. In my eyes, the information I pull on Realtor complements the data I get off Zillow. Here I can find square footage, price-per-square foot, school districts, heating and cooling equipment in the structure and so on. You can even find the year the structure was built.

Another website I use is **Trulia.com**. Trulia embeds school ratings information into each listings and the site includes a nice mortgage calculator that permits you to play with figures to estimate and plan your mortgage payments to service your debt.

Next I visit **Neighborhoodscout.com**. Neighborhoodscout has incredibly useful information. The **description tab** describes the neighborhood in great detail. It includes information on demographics and crucial **vacancy rates** for the neighborhood as a whole. If you forget to check something, don't forget to check vacancy rates because a **high vacancy rate increase your risk substantially**. If your goal is to rent out a structure at the present time or sometime in the future, do not sign a purchase agreement until you study the neighborhood's vacancy rate.

After that, go to Spotcrime.com. This website gives you a feel for safety. It tracks criminal activity of all types and plots it on Google Maps. A high threat neighborhood for crime will turn off most tenants and make your property harder to sell.

What makes a good deal? A good deal is priced significantly below present market value, in a good, safe location for the target market you want to rent to, with decent schools. Other factors to consider are demographics, crime rates, vacancy rates and proximity to child predators. All of these are considerations tenants care about and so should you. Ultimately, when you feel like you are sitting on a good deal, ask yourself this question.

Would I live there? If you answer no, save your money, forget the hours you spent analyzing the data and walk away. The truth is another deal is always just around

the corner.

Chapter 3

Real estate is my life. It is my day job, if you will. But it consumes my nights and weekends too.

- Ivanka Trump

What kind of real estate should I buy? Existing homes vs. New Construction?

I will never buy a new home again. I'll explain why. My first real estate purchase ever was new construction. It was an invaluable learning experience for me. The chief lesson I learned was the price of a new home isn't the price of a new home. Normally, the sales price of a new home just includes the existing structure and the land. But what about all the necessities not included in the price? I'm talking about things like appliances, window blinds and sod. I'm talking about things like a garage door opener, security system and irrigation system. The list goes on and on. It's like buying a new car. A new home is the base model. You will need to pay extra for the upgrades. If you purchase these upgrades through home builder, prepare yourself to pay premium prices for low quality materials. You shouldn't be upset with the builder because of this. It's just business and business is about profits. Overall, you will do much better coordinating any upgrades yourself. Over time, you will develop a nice library of business contacts that will benefit you as you make future acquisitions. Building a network of reliable, affordable maintenance contractors is vital to success in the real estate business.

There are other reasons I avoid new construction. Land settles over time. Although modern foundation construction techniques reduce the risk of foundation problems due to settling - some risk still exists. Additionally, new construction is simply more costly than existing homes in most cases. Brand new materials and modern floor plans cost top dollar. Architecture, interior design, and advertising costs are significantly higher. When you purchase an existing home, these expenses where shouldered by someone else.

Although, I favor purchasing existing homes over new homes, the age of the home is still critical. **An ideal acquisition is 5 - 15 years old.** Using this range, you are purchasing a home with a relatively modern floor plan without the new home price. A contemporary floor plan is crucial. People are a trendy species. People flock to what is hot, hip and popular. At this moment, one of the most popular handbags for women in Michael Kors. A tiny handbag that holds a small wallet and a tube of lipstick costs over $300. People pick homes their same way. If granite countertops are trendy, people will want them. If beige carpets are the rave, people will rush to rent your home if you have them. If every builder is building large 4 bedrooms with 2 baths, it's because this floor plan is hot! You must keep abreast of what is contemporary in floor plans, lightning and interior design and make your acquisitions based on current trends. By picking homes, 5 - 15 years old, you will get the best of both worlds - relatively modern floors at a reasonable price.

For quick reference purposes and to exercise critical thought, here is a table of the advantages and disadvantages of purchasing new vs. existing homes.

New Homes

Advantages	Disadvantages
Home warranty	Higher cost-per-square foot
Less routine maintenance issues	Neighborhood not established
Long life span for major systems (i.e. roof, central	Land is still settling

heat/air, electrical, plumbing)	
Modern floor plans	Amenities/upgrades costs not included (i.e. sod, window blinds, appliances, etc.)

Existing Homes

Advantages	Disadvantages
Lower cost-per-square foot	Age of major systems (roof, central heat/air, electrical, plumbing)
Established neighborhoods	Outdated floor plans
Amenities/Upgrades included (i.e. sod, window blinds, appliances, etc.)	Home warranty not included (Note: Sometimes these warranty can be purchased at additional cost)
Settled foundation	Constant routine maintenance

Overall, I feel the advantages of purchasing existing homes outweigh the benefits of purchasing new homes. In my experience, I've been able to purchase existing homes significantly under market value. New homes are always purchased at market value. Home builders are reluctant to haggle over their asking price because they must protect the asking price of their other vacant homes for sale. Market value changes significantly if builders accepts a lower price and that doesn't make business sense.

Existing homes carry a lower cost-per-square foot and amenities like window blinds, sod and appliances are often already included. This shortens the time from acquisition to market resulting in a shorter turnover time and your investment dollars are returned to you faster.

Existing homes can be purchased via online auction or through foreclosure asset managers while new homes are only purchased at full market value through new home builders. Often, the amount of potential income between new and existing structures is insignificant and do not justify the larger costs of brand new construction.

I have centered my own personal strategy on existing homes and I recommend you do too. If your acquisitions are well-selected, they are permanent in their value and income.

Chapter 4

Real estate investing, even on a very small scale, remains a tried and true means of building an individual's cash flow and wealth.

- Robert Kiyosaki

Should I buy residential or commercial real estate?

What is your investment strategy? Should you invest in residential or commercial real estate? These are very important questions that deserve a lot of critical thought and attention. But before you can answer these questions you need to know the difference between the two investment vehicles.

Residential real estate is normally defined as single-family homes by most experts. Residential real estate has a clear advantage. Let's look at the benefit of residential real estate investing.

The most obvious benefit is everyone across this world needs some type of shelter from the elements if they are to survive. Considering this, residential real estate is immune to technological advances. There is no technological advancement or invention that will make a human's need for shelter obsolete. Humanity's survival depends on residential real estate. Therefore it is one of the safest investments around. Residential real estate has been a proven investment since the beginning of time. Now let's examine commercial real estate.

Commercial real estate is considered by most as real land used for commercial purposes. What does that mean? Perhaps I should clarify with some examples. Commercial real estate is land/buildings like shopping malls, office parks, gas stations, car washes, restaurants, hotels, etc. What is the greatest advantage of commercial real estate?

The greatest advantage is long-term leases. If a Taco Bell leases your commercial property and the business is successful, barring some strange turn of events you can expect to keep that tenant for decades as long as the business continues to thrive and grow. Corporations usually negotiate automatic rent increases over time in the lease too. These corporations know location is everything and they want to keep property owners happy. We've discussed residential and commercial real estate but we've left off one important type of property - multi-family real estate. What is multi-family real estate? What asset class does multi-family real estate fit in?

Multi-family real estate are your duplexes and apartment buildings. It is simply a structure occupied by multiple families. I categorize multi-family property as commercial rather than residential and I'll explain why. Single-family real estate encourages long-term tenant occupancy. The design of these structures are the chief driving factors. A home is built for a single family. There are spaces for outdoor recreation in form of front/back yards. These structures are sometimes quaint but private. Tenants simply tend to be happier in single-family homes. Apartment buildings are much different.

Apartment buildings are about minimal space for maximum profit. The building itself is built with efficiency in mind. Small rooms, small bathrooms supporting multiple families under a shared roof. After living in apartment buildings at various points in my life, I think most people view them as short term solutions to their housing needs. Apartments are noisy, cramped and less private. Tenants migrate in and out of these units. If anyone has a choice, only a relative few would select an apartment for permanent housing needs. Apartments feel like motels to me and I would think most people agree with me. I classify apartment buildings the same way I classify motels - commercial real estate.

Now that we understand the difference between commercial and residential real estate, we need to examine the most important questions of all. Which one is better? Which one do I choose?

The answer is both.

Residential real estate is a fantastic investment if purchased at the right price. Residential real estate typically attracts families and families tend to stay in home longer. Families are reluctant to uproot children from schools and friends so expect long-term leases with these structures. However, everything isn't completely rosy with residential real estate. Most of the time, residential real estate produce lower profits when compared to commercial real estate. Most people that get into residential real estate leave frustrated and discouraged from years of negative cash flow. Does this mean you should avoid residential real estate - absolutely not. However, you need to purchase these structures at the right price and expect lower positive cash flow after expenses.

Do you need significant positive cash flow now? If the answer is yes - you might favor commercial real estate. Most people will dive into commercial real estate by purchasing a building so I need to address the pros and cons of these structures.

Apartment building will produce nice positive cash flow if you can get the structure 100% occupied. That's *if* you can get it occupied. If most people have a choice, they will pick a home over an apartment every time. People are social beings but people adore privacy too. There simply isn't any real privacy in an apartment building. *If* you can manage to get tenants, don't expect them to stay long. Apartment buildings are stepping stones not permanent solutions to a person's long-term housing needs. As soon as they are financially able, they are going to get a house. So what's the best strategy with apartment buildings? Target a market that will stay in the apartment for a long time. This is normally low income people getting government vouchers. Their housing options are limited since many property owners are unwilling to accept government vouchers due to bureaucratic red tape and a negative stigma to the program and its benefactors. Considering that, these tenants will likely stay awhile and reduce your vacancy/turnover rate.

This gets back to our question. Which asset class is best? Should I buy and hold residential or commercial real estate? You need all types to diversify and limit your risk. Like all markets, real estate markets fluctuate based off current economic conditions. At times residential real estate will be hot. Other times, residential real estate will be colder than the center of a microwave burrito. A portfolio of different real estate assets will balance your holdings and limit your risk. If your residential house isn't renting, hopefully your apartment building is picking up the slack. If your apartment building isn't performing well perhaps the rent you collect from the restaurant owner renting your building on Main Street will. Just like in stocks, diversity saves you from losing it all. In real estate diversity functions the same way. **As you build your real estate empire, ensure you branch out in other real estate asset classes.** I don't know one person who has achieved permanent success by putting all their eggs in one basket.

Chapter 5

Real estate was perfect training for going into public life because you learn to accept rejection, learn to work with people and find common ground. That's the way you sell houses...that's also the way you win over constituency.

- Johnny Isakson

How do I finance deals?

By now you understand the benefits of real estate investing. By now you know the strengths and weaknesses of the business. You understand the different types of structures. You understand what a good deal is. Now, the question arises. How do I finance deals? Over the next chapter, we will look at different financing options and point out some things to look out for with each one.

Cash

Cash is king! Cash is a fantastic way to purchase real estate but most people simply don't have $50,000 to $100,000 just laying around. However, if you do have cash available, you can get some incredible deals on real estate. Why? First, closing costs are much lower on a cash purchase. This turns into negotiating power for you. With a cash purchase a survey isn't required...no mortgage loan closing costs...no points...no costs associated with financing a loan. A cash purchase gives you incredible power to really negotiate a great deal. If you are purchasing a foreclosure or a short sell, asset managers are very interested in you because they are certain the deal will close. Cash has always equaled power in our society and it is no different concerning real estate. Lastly, lenders are reluctant to lend on a property needing serious rehab. For lenders, the appraisal is key to how much risk they will assume. Therefore, if the property doesn't appraise for over the loan amount you can forget about a loan. However, you can pick up a significant rehab for tens of thousands under market value. At times, these structures can be restored to the former glory and you can pocket a fat profit. I've made more money in a single deal than most people make all year. Remember, significant rehabs are an all-cash business transaction. Keep that in mind if you plan to use this approach to real estate investing as part of your game plan.

Borrowing Money

If you are like most people, a full cash purchase is out of reach. What do you do now? It's simple. You save. If you don't have the ability to make a full cash purchase save your money for a sizable down-payment on your purchase. The down-payment needs to be large enough to provide positive cash flow after you service your mortgage. If you are using your real estate purchase for investment reasons - meaning you aren't going to live in it. Most banks will require at least 25% down. I would shoot for 30%. You will be attempted to spend your monthly surplus on some luxuries. I'd resist that if I were you. You should save your monthly surplus until you have enough to fund another acquisition. Using this strategy, you will grow a notable real estate empire over the decades.

A Combined Approach

The fastest way to grow an empire is using a combined approach. Using this strategy, you save and purchase your first home with a full cash. Using this home as collateral, you immediately borrow as much as possible effectively returning most of the money you just paid into the home. This provides liquid cash you can use to fund your next purchase. I have a friend that uses this method and he has amassed 31 properties with it. You can really grow an empire fast but this method carries a lot of risk. Lenders will likely only give you a variable rate using this method. If interest rates move considerably upward, your house of cards will crumble. In short, your real estate empire is built off debt so it is vulnerable.

As for me, I like a combined approach but I check my growth and keep my empire manageable. If you look to the past, history is loaded with examples of failed empires that tried to grow too fast. Real estate is no different. An empire built on debt is just a stack of cards waiting for the right catalyst to make it fall. However, debt is a power too. It is absolutely impossible to create significant wealth in a single lifetime without it. I balance my debt with liquid cash. This means I have an amount of cash equal to my current debt load just sitting in an account ready to pay off my debts at a moment's notice, if needed. This checks my growth and limits my risk too.

The dilemma of risk vs. reward has challenged and tempted mankind since the beginning of time. I wish there was an easy answer to the question of risk vs.

reward but there isn't one. You must determine your own level of risk and execute your real estate strategy based on it.

Chapter 6

A funny thing happens in real estate. When it comes back, it comes back up like gangbusters.

-Barbara Corcoran

Making Offers

I'm going to start this chapter off by discussing one of the most fascinating words in the English vocabulary. It is a word you already know but seldom think about. This single word can bring us untold riches yet when this word materializes itself in our lives, the vast majority of us shrink back from its potential power - overpowered by its shroud of uncertainty and risk. What is this word that both tempts and torments mankind? The word is opportunity.

A leading online dictionary defines opportunity as "a set of circumstances that makes it possible to do something." The key word in this definition is *possible*. The word possible hints at a hidden assumption that everyone already knows. In *opportunity hides risk*. Hidden deep into the ocean of possible profits lies the threat of significant risk. It is the quality of opportunity that holds us back from reaching our full potential. Overall, mankind fears risk. Sure, there is a very small portion of society that embraces risk. These people are your daredevils. These are your thrill-seekers that climb the Himalayas, bungee jump off the steepest cliffs and ride barrels over the largest waterfalls. Yes, the world has a small percentage of these types of daring personalities but the rest of us fear risk. It's hard to explain why this risk-averse quality is a part of us. Everyone has their theories but, the truth is, no one really knows. This quality is just there. It is the fear of risk that causes us to miss opportunity.

It calls on us to **NOT** take action, when we should. It whispers to us with faulty logic and deceit. It is a staunch debater countering all our pros with false cons unsupported by data. In the end, we sit and watch opportunity pass by. We sit and watch opportunity fatten another person's wallet.

I will tell you a simple truth. **In real estate, the best deals pass by quickly.** In other words, in real estate, opportunity passes by quickly. In order for you to seize opportunity, you must learn to lock up real estate to prevent others from buying it. You lock up real estate with contracts. Sometimes these contracts are referred to simply as Purchase Agreements. **A purchase agreement is just a written agreement between a buyer and a seller that dictates and details the terms and conditions related to the terms and conditions to the purchase and sale of an asset.** In other words, it is a simple piece of paper and it is nothing to fear. In fact, you must learn to exploit its power and protection.

A purchase agreement protects the buyer and seller simultaneously. It protects them both in numerous ways.

1. A purchase agreement prevents the seller from accepting a higher bid on their property. For example, suppose you have an accepted contract to purchase 123 Memory Lane for $150,000. What if two days later, another buyer offers $200,000 to purchase 123 Memory Lane? The answer is nothing. The seller must sell 123 Memory Lane to you since you have a written contract. A written contract is your muscle. It is your enforcer and it protects the buyer and it forces the seller to keep their word.
2. A purchase agreement protects the seller too. Suppose the seller has an accepted contract to sell 123 Memory Lane for $150,000. What prevents the buyer from continuing to shop around for a better deal? The contract does. If the buyer fails to fulfil his promise to the seller, he is likely to be sued. Your purchase agreement is similar to a marriage; once you are in it, you are stuck! And just like a marriage, it takes some work to get out of one.

Purchase agreements may seem scary to new real estate investors but they really aren't. The truth is purchase agreements are powerful tools. I use these documents to seize opportunities and lock up real estate. And if you are smart and careful, there are ways you can weasel out of the deal later. I'll show you how.

The first way is by giving up your earnest money. **Earnest money is a deposit that shows the seller that a buyer is serious and sincere about purchasing a piece of real estate.** When the deal is finalized, the money is put towards the buyer's down payment. If the deal falls apart, the seller keeps the earnest money.

The amount of earnest money required to lock up a property is 100% negotiable. As a buyer, you want to get the earnest deposit as low as you can get it, just in case a deal falls apart. This limits your potential losses. As a seller, you want to demand the highest amount of earnest money you can. This compensates you for the precious time your home is off the market. The fact is you are missing opportunities when your home is locked up by a contract.

The second way you can legally weasel out of a real estate deal is with contingency clauses. **A contingency clause is a clause that allows cancellation of a contract without penalty if a certain event happens or fails to happen.** The most common contingency clauses are for repair costs and financing. Contingency clauses are powerful and they are virtually a risk-free way to lock up real estate and prevent a missed opportunity. I'll explain how I use them.

My favorite contingency clause is the repair clause. I try to get the repair contingency clause as low as I can. In most cases, I get it for a few hundred dollars. With a repair contingency that low, it gives me a free pass to walk away from any deal free of charge because any home inspector, in their right mind, will find at least $300 dollars of repairs on a property. Unless the home is immaculate, repair contingency clauses give you a get out of jail free card.

I've given you the basics of making an offer and I've taught you how to lock up real estate. In the next chapter, we will explore in greater detail, the timeless debate of whether or not, you should purchase your real estate holding with

cash.

Chapter 7

Increasingly, the real estate developers can't get bank loans for their project financing in China. They're now going into the Hong Kong market to raise money in the bond market at very, very high rates, as high as 15, 20 percent.

- James Chanos

Should You Really Buy With Cash?

Why do you think I started off this chapter with that quote? Is it because I think the Chinese real estate market is the next big thing? No. It's because I want to highlight the risks of using leverage, also known as debt, for financing real estate purchases. When you purchase properties with leverage, you are a slave to the interest rate. The interest rate can make you or break you.

A low interest rate may equate into profitability and a nice monthly stipend for your bank account. A high interest rate surely will not. A good real estate investment using leverage is brought at the right price and financed at the right interest rate. Using leverage to fund real estate is risky; using cash reduces this risk considerably. That is why I love to use cash to fund most of my real estate investments. How do I do it? I simply save.

Every month my holdings generate cash profits. Instead of spending these profits on a new car or a trip to Europe I simply invest the money into stock and bond accounts. The regular monthly profits combine with a nice annual return and my pot of cash grows in no time. Normally, I'm ready to fund a cash purchase every two years, depending on my rate of return. I have to be 100% honest. I don't fund all of my real estate purchases with cash. I use a little leverage too. Here is my strategy. I keep $200,000 sitting in a stock account. I limit my leverage to that amount. In an extreme emergency, I can quickly liquidate this account and pay off all my debt in a heartbeat. In a sense, I'm using leverage virtually risk-free.

Tenants labor for me and pay off my mortgage while I watch it all happen. If I get in a financial bind, I can liquidate and be back to my debt-free self within a few days.

Ultimately, cash is king. I use it to fund the vast majority of my purchases but leverage is an incredible power because it lets you tap into the labor of others. Leverage permits others to work for you and this is something you cannot duplicate with cash.

In this short chapter I have given you my thoughts on purchasing real estate with cash. In the next one, I will tell you why I favor buying and holding real estate over every other real estate investing strategy.

Chapter 8

I want to be a successful landlord. I like real estate.

- Two Chainz

Buying and Holding Real Estate - What you need to know

I wrote my first book **"Get Rich Off A Minimum Wage Income"** a few years ago. In that book, I discussed the importance of doing great research and analysis prior to buying stock investments. In that book, I encouraged readers to buy and hold sound deals forever. Real estate is no different. Currently, there are plenty of other real estate investing strategies out there such as flipping properties and offering properties rent to own but out of all the strategies, buying and holding is the most effective. There are a few reasons for this.

First, the transaction costs of buying and holding real estate are expensive. Currently, on average, you will drop 6% of the sales price of your property just to pay the realtors (buyers/sellers). This doesn't include other expenses such survey, title insurance, points of a mortgage loan and a home warranty. Ultimately, once you do the math, you spend a lot of your home equity just to sell or purchase a home. The transactions fees are just the tip of the iceberg. You must pay short-term capital gains tax too! Yes, Uncle Sam gets his cut anytime money changes hands in America. If you happen to make a profit after paying the realtors and the closing costs. Uncle Sam will tax what's left at 25% adding insult to injury. If flipping is your strategy, you have a lot of obstacles to overcome to realize profitable deals. That's is why I think flipping is a doomed strategy.

Now, let's look at "rent to own" strategies. This is very similar to leasing a car. Using this strategy, sellers charge rent that is higher than market rate. The market rate rent is given to the seller as monthly rent while the surplus is stashed in a slush fund to build a buyer's down payment over the lease period. At the end of the lease, the buyer can use that money as a down payment to purchase the home. Sounds great for both parties right? Not exactly. The contracts with these types of deals can be legal cesspools. Many buyers have been cheated out of their hard earned money with legal loopholes designed to cheat low income people out of their money. I avoid "rent to own" strategies at all costs. These strategies prey of the low income because it is very likely these hopeful buyers will pay above market rent for a number of years and lose their entire savings prior to closing the deal due to a legal loophole. This is the ethical dilemma you are faced with rent to own strategies.

I believe business is based on mutual benefit. I provide a good or service that is useful to you and your provide me some income. If both parties aren't satisfied at the end of the deal, we didn't conduct business. In my mind, true business is a win-win situation. It is important that I sleep well at night. I can't sleep well knowing I struck a contract with a low income family that I know they cannot fulfil. This is the vast majority of "rent to own" strategies and this is why I avoid them altogether.

Buying and holding a property is the way to go and here's why.

In most circumstances, real estate increases in value over time when purchased at a reasonable price. The trick here is to purchase real estate at a reasonable price. You must avoid market bubbles at all costs. If everyone is purchasing real estate at the moment, should you? No! Market prices are set by the market conditions of supply and demand. If demand is high, real estate prices rise in response. Periods of high demand equal high prices and the real estate investor may not pay a fair price for a parcel of real estate in this type of overheated market. However, if purchased at the right price under ideal market conditions, the value of your real estate acquisition will grow over time. Even though the value of real estate rises over time, there is another reason why buying and holding real estate makes sense. I will sum it up in one word. **Income.**

You will be hard pressed to find another investment that produces as much income as real estate. I think the only investment that will produce more on a monthly basis is owning your own business. However, owning your own business includes a lot of headaches most people don't want. There are marketing problems, personnel problems, inventory problems, fulfillment problems and a whole host of other issues I'm not going to mention here. I'd have to write another book to list them all. Normally, owning real estate is less complex and a wisely chosen property can pay for itself in five to six years. The trick is picking your property wisely. It needs to be purchased with cash significantly under market value to leave you room to make improvements or updates the property. Don't forget about the location too. At a minimum, I only buy properties that will produce enough income to equal 20% of the market purchase price per year. For example, if I purchase a home for $50,000, it must produce at least $10,000 in rental income per year. Remember, to consider a projected vacancy rate. At the time of this writing, the U.S. average is 6.49% and this is a point in time snapshot. The average vacancy rate varies depending on state and city. For example, at the time of this writing, the U.S. Census department, states average vacancy rate is 7.86% in the state of Texas. This figure is over 1% higher than the national average. In real estate, small numbers matter and you must do a detailed analysis of any property you plan to purchase and the conditions of the real estate market the property is located in.

My last word on income. Cash is king and you will be hard pressed to find another

investment that produces more cash on a monthly basis than real estate.

Chapter 9

"If you think hiring a pro is expensive wait till you hire an amateur."

- Red Adair

Should you do it yourself or hire a property manager?

Should you manage your properties yourself or not? This has always been a hotly debated topic. There are pros and cons to each approach. Let's start with doing it yourself.

Obviously, managing property yourself is cheaper and it will put more money in your pocket on a monthly basis. In most locations, the standard fee for hiring a property manager is 10% of the monthly rent. Although, this is negotiable, I must caution you with going with the lowest bidder. Hiring top talent, simply costs money and it is worth paying for. Very often, new real estate investors make the mistake of hiring low quality property managers and it comes back to bite them in the butt. I did it myself when I first started. I simply focused on the lowest bidder. It didn't thoroughly investigate their experience and qualifications. I didn't ask about their proposed marketing plan or tenant screening process. I didn't inquire about property inspections or accounting. I was a newbie and I made newbie mistakes. I hired low quality talent simply because it was cheap. I had to fire this property manager after my property sat vacant for months and I had a series of mismanagement failures to include vandalism to my property because the property manager left the door unsecured. It was a disaster but I learned a priceless lesson. You have to pay for top talent. The best property managers simply won't work cheap and this statement is true across every profession. In my case, I have more money than I will ever need and I simply won't work cheap either. I'd rather not work at all than be paid less than I'm worth. In some cases, property management fees don't stop with simply the monthly commission. Sometimes, property management companies charge additional marketing fees, leasing fees, vacancy fees and more.

Here's my take on all these nickel and dime fees. If the property management company wants to charge you these fees, find another property management company. **It is the property management company's job to get your property rented!** If you are paying your property management company a vacancy fee, you are paying them to sit on their butt! I wanted to use another word but I want this to be a book my kids can read. Sorry, I don't tolerate laziness and vacancy fees are the epitome of laziness. I believe these fees promote laziness! Just think about it, the property manager can collect a $25 a month vacancy fee and do nothing at all for your property.

Leasing fees are equally annoying. Leasing fees are an additional fee a property manager collects simply for getting your property leased. Last time I checked, it was their job to get your property leased! If the property manager is collecting a leasing fee, what is the monthly commission for? The top property management firms won't nickel and dime you with these silly additional fees. Their goal is to make you money and keep you satisfied so you'll come back with repeat business. It should be your goal to provide an exceptional product to your tenants too because the same rules apply. If you take care of your tenants, they will take care of you and your property.

Another drawback of professional property management is you normally lose control of tenant screening. In most cases, you have no idea of who gets to rent your property. You have no idea of their credit history and you are not normally privy to the results of their background check. For some real estate investors this hands-off approach is actually an incredible benefit. The day-to-day management of the property is more of a chore and not actually fun for these investors. However, in the case of tenant screening, I think this task is not that important for you to oversee as an real estate investor if you hire the right property manager. The important point to note here is you must hire the right property manager. Another critical point is you must quickly fire the company if you make a mistake and misjudged their talent. As a real estate investor, you are a business owner and it is a job not for the faint of heart. Sometimes you have to fire a management firm for poor performance. If you will hesitate to take this action, please don't get into real estate investing. Go with a nice, diversified mutual fund instead. You have less gray hairs in the end.

What is my advice to you? Hire a professional or do it yourself? My answer is...it depends. Let me elaborate. When you first start real estate investing, you will be a small fry. You will have one or two properties and it is reasonable you can manage your small holdings yourself. You can keep a full-time job and still market your properties, conduct tenant screening and coordinate repairs. After you grow your holdings, things become more complicated. Your daily burden grows significantly. You'll need to respond to tenant concerns, advertise your vacant units, coordinate maintenance and perform bookkeeping. Your tax planning becomes more complex too. All of these daily activities will keep you from doing what you do best...finding and taking action on new emergent deals. All of these daily activities will really cut into your leisure time too. Who really wants their cell phone going off at 10 p.m. at night because a tenant locked themselves out of their apartment? In my case, I started managing my properties myself until I found a fantastic real estate management company. Since I bought multiple properties to the table, I negotiated control of several functions I simply didn't want to give up. I still control setting rent price and tenant screening. I use my own contractor for repairs too. At this point, I manage the property manager while they manage my units. I couldn't ask for a better relationship because I love leisure

activities. Now, I have plenty of time for these activities.

Chapter 10

"I never dreamed about success. I worked for it."

- Estee Lauder

Putting it all together

I'm 100% retired at 42 years old. I take that back. I suppose I'm self-employed. I'm a full-time investor. However, I work when I want to. It's a wonderful life. I'm able to exercise regularly and engage in a variety of social activities at my choosing. It is true freedom. A typical day for me looks this.

I wake up when I want and I surf the internet looking for stock and real estate deals. I like to use websites with powerful tools so I can sort companies based on valuation statistics. For real estate, I like to use websites that I can sort properties based on market value. I limit my search to blue-collar neighborhoods within my target price range of $50,000 to $80,000.

One of the key items, I look for is instant equity. In other words, I must find a property at least $20,000 or more below current market value. If I don't find one that meets this minimum criteria, I simply walk away and go enjoy some leisure activities. In other words, I call my work day complete despite only working less than an hour.

Additionally, since I'm a buy and hold investor, I assess how much rent I could get for the place. A purchase has to makes sense. I'm looking for three things here.

1. I want to know possible market monthly rent rate.

2. I want to know the properties' capitalization rate.
3. I want to know my return on investment measured in years.

I compute the market monthly rent simply by finding a similar property and seeing what it rents for. The monthly rent rate is an important figure. It's critical you assess this accurately since it is the basis for all your other computations. What happens if you can't find a similar property with a similar amount of bedrooms or square footage? No problem. You simply find any nearby property and compute the monthly rent rate per square foot by dividing the rent price by the square footage. For example, suppose there is a two bedroom apartment that is 1200 square foot renting for $650 a month. If you do the math, you'll find it is renting for $.54 per square foot. Now you can apply the "price per square foot" to your own property. Let's assume your property is a one bedroom apartment that is 1100 square foot. How much could this property earn you in monthly income? If you multiply $.54 by 1100, you will get $595. In theory, your property should earn you $595 per month based on market conditions/price-per-square foot.

There are some weaknesses to this computation. It completely ignores human emotion and focuses solely on market conditions. You will find some renters will pay considerably more money for amenities like granite kitchen countertops or a fireplace. I completely ignore these amenities because they are personality driven and my goal is to get a property occupied quickly with a good tenant. It's vital you hold out for a good qualified tenant. Anytime you place a tenant into a property they can't afford, you are asking for trouble. You aren't doing the tenant any favors by permitting them to live above their means and you are almost certainly going to incur additional legal expenses since you will likely have to evict your tenant for non-payment of rent some day. Do yourself a favor and hold out for a good, qualified tenant.

Next is a properties' capitalization rate.

Let's assume, I find a potential deal that meets my criteria. What do I do next? I pick up the phone and call my realtor.

My realtor is not your average realtor. This guy owns over 30 properties of his own and he has decades of experience. I tell him I found a potential gem and I'd like to see it as soon as possible. In real estate, it's all about speed because if it is a good deal, you will have a lot of competition to secure this property by getting it under contract.

After I meet him at the property, we perform a joint inspection. If possible, we assess the major systems like plumbing, electrical, HVAC and foundation. This initial property inspection serves two purposes.

1. It lets me know if an investment has value.
2. It lets me estimate repair or rehab costs.

In real estate, I think properties near schools or parks have a lot of value. I find these properties highly desirable and I seek these sort of amenities to ease my vacancy rates. I find people tend to like centrally located properties close to shopping and restaurants. If a military base is nearby, you'll find military members like properties close to their base. Apartment buildings near colleges are very desirable. Waterfront properties and cul de sac homes have incredible value too.

Estimating maintenance costs takes experience. Over time, you'll build a network of maintenance professionals. By conducting regular business with them, you will commit to memory how much certain repairs will cost you. For example, at the time of this writing, I know to lay ceramic tile over roughly 600 sq feet will cost me about $1300 in labor and about $600 in materials in my market. I have a licensed electrician that will replace outlets and switches for $5.00 each. I have a handyman that installs ceiling fans for $50 per fan. Painting, roofing, appliances, whatever - I know who to call. Over time so will you.

After I estimate the repair costs, I lock in my investment by putting a contract on it. On every contract unless you are ready to take some significant risk, you need to get title insurance. You can ask the seller to pay for it. Sometimes the seller will, other times not. It depends on the deal but it never hurts to ask. The contract should have a method for you to weasel out of the deal based on a contingency. These are called contingency clauses. Most realtors will write in a contingency clause based on a dollar amount for repairs. For example, we may write in a contingency clause for repairs exceeding $500. In this case, if a property inspector finds I have $600 in repairs, I can simply walk away from the contract with no questions asked. Asset managers for foreclosures or repos will not let you normally include such a contingency clause in a contract. The asset is normally priced well-below market value with the idea the buyer will need to make many necessary repairs. Additionally, foreclosures and repos cost the asset manager's company money. For example, property taxes still must be paid. Perhaps, the utilities are on. Organizations with repos and foreclosures still have to protect what value the assets have left. Therefore companies will usually incur costs to winterize their real estate holdings when a freeze is expected. Given this hemorrhaging of funds, sometimes asset managers want to just get rid of properties. During these times, you can secure valuable real estate for tens of thousands under market.

Lastly, I like to know my return-on-investment or ROI. I simply want to know when I will make my money back. ROI is simple to calculate. You take your projected annual revenue and divide it by the purchase price of the home. For example, let's suppose you pay cash for a single-family home that cost $100,000. Let's project you can rent this property for $1000 per month resulting in $12,000 in revenue for the year. If you divide $100,000 / $12,000 - your return on investment is 8.3 years. In a little over 8 years, you will get everything you put into the home and the rest from that point is pure profits. You need to understand ROI has some weaknesses. This simplified formula for ROI assumes no expenses such as management fees or maintenance. You can manage a property yourself if you like but you are definitely going to incur some maintenance fees over the cost of a given year so you'll be wise to estimate annual maintenance and reduce your annual revenue accordingly. Additionally, don't forget mortgage costs if you plan to purchase your holdings with debt. The important thing here is you need to make sure a purchase is profitable and not taking money out of your wallet or purse monthly. **A good real estate purchase adds money to your pockets every month!**

Once you find a good property, lock it up with a contract, purchase it and rehab it. You place your new asset into the market. You need to understand this is where the competition starts. You are competing against every rental house in your neighborhood and you are competing against every property across the city at your price range. Here is where you need to pursue competitive advantage. Ultimately, you have to bring to the market the most appealing property at the best price. How will you do this? It's really the little things that set your property apart from your competition. Sometimes it's faux wood blinds, granite countertops, new carpet, deep stainless steel sinks, modern appliances or curb appeal. You need to scout out your competition. Call and inquire about properties for rent near your own. Ask about rental price and amenities. How does your own property compare? What if every home you are competing against has a garbage disposal and you don't? You can expect your property to go unrented. Business is tough and only the strong survive.

You may be tempted to undercut your competition. I suggest you do not do this. Let's say single-family homes in your neighborhood rent for $1200 per month. In an effort to rent your home quickly, you may list yours for $1100 per month. Why is this a bad idea? The market rate rent price protects your entire neighborhood. If you start to lower your rent price, your competition may pursue the same strategy and the whole dynamics of the neighborhood can change. I've seen this happen in a very short time period too. Price wars in this manner are very bad for business. Not only will you reduce your monthly income, you may significantly lower the overall value of your properties. It is better to price your property slightly higher than market in an effort to raise the rental prices, property values and overall quality of a neighborhood.

Putting it all together is not hard. The hard part is going for it. It is not easy to assume $300,000 in debt with no guarantee of success. However, risk is the American way and with great risk comes great reward.

I cannot close out a book without some words of wisdom. This is compilation of tidbits I've learned over the years of working in real estate and working with some awesome real estate professionals.

Networking is key - Networking is the key to success in the real estate business. A lot of times it happens by luck, chance and circumstance. Sometimes you need to be proactive. In my case, I met the President of a large brokerage firm simply by chance. I was purchasing my home with cash and he heard about it and wanted to meet me. We hit it off and we quickly became friends. From there the rest is history. He is my personal realtor and he makes fairly easy commissions on large purchases. I still profit from his wisdom and guidance. Additionally, he has introduced me to every major player in real estate in the city that I operate in. I know all the best contractors and I get preferred customer pricing. This special pricing puts more money in my pocket allowing me to do what I do best - find good deals with hidden value!

If you need to be proactive, do it! My mentor and I regularly attend real estate auctions. Once, as we departed from an auction, we were stopped by a young realtor just starting out. He introduced himself and gave a nice 30 second brief on himself and his business. It was well rehearsed and well received by us. He made a good first impression. It's not hard to find out who the movers and shakers in real estate are. It's all public record and their names including all their properties are held in the city archives.

Never buy brand new - I don't buy brand new properties. The real key to building incredible wealth is never pay full market price for anything. When you buy brand new, you are immediately paying full market price. If you aren't a savvy negotiator, you may pay over market value by missing out on free upgrades like sod, privacy fencing and more. Real estate is a numbers game and the numbers hardly make sense with a new purchase. You will have to deal with new building issues too like settling. And no one knows what the neighborhood will ultimately become in the long run. These are the pitfalls of buying brand new and that is why I avoid new properties. Just pretend you are a shopper at your local discount store and hunt for your purchases in the bargain aisle.

Stay away from the oldest buildings - I never buy new and I never buy really old either. When I first started real estate investing, my very first purchase was a home built in 1962. I was introduced to a vast array of "old house problems". The water pipes were galvanized steel and a pipe burst on me and flooded the whole crawl space. This buckled the entire wood floor and caused mold problems too. Ultimately, the floor had to be replaced along with the water pipes costing over ten thousand dollars. An older home may have a floor plan unsuitable to modern taste too. Older floor usually close off the kitchen and limit the flow of natural light as opposed to modern, open floor plans. If you purchase an older home, you can expect to budget for new electrical wiring, water pipes, windows and insulation. In most cases, the cabinetry is outdated and will need replacing or refinishing. Nine times out of ten, a purchase of an older home simply isn't worth it. Now, having said that, I know investors who routinely purchase older homes and make a lot of money off them. How do they do it? They simply do the bare minimum to the property and get a low-income tenant in it. In short, they slumlord the property out. That is a business I want no part of. Ultimately, when it is all said and done, nothing goes with us when we die. We are only care-takers of the assets we think we own. I want to pass away knowing I cared for the assets entrusted to me well. I want to know I left the buildings in better condition than when I received them. I want to know I provided someone a wonderful place to live. I want to know that I enriched an entire neighborhood. I want to know that I worked to make the world a better place. I frown my nose at slumlords and I shun the practice.

Analyze your target market - I spend considerable time thinking about the customers I'd like to attract to my properties. Think about the following questions when you view a property. Who will likely want to rent or buy this home in the future? What are the baseline amenities expected from your target market? What does your nearby competition offer? How will you advertise this property to your target market? Answering these questions will take you through the process of analyzing your target market. A detailed analysis will substantially reduced your risk and exponentially raise your likelihood of success while a substandard analysis could give you a one-way ticket to the poor house. Analyzing your target market is important. It is one of the most important functions of real estate investing.

Create a business plan - Many people hate writing business plans but I feel it is a necessary evil. By writing a business plan, you are forced to critically think about your business, your products, your competitors, your marketing, your finances and your customers. You are forced to think strategically. A business plan can keep you focused too. Let's suppose your business plan states you will purchase, own and operate only single-family residences and you are presented with an opportunity to own a multi-family building. What should you do? Walk away from the deal? Maybe or maybe not. The point is a business plan should force you to think long and hard about any emergent opportunity not addressed by the plan. In short, a good business plan forces you to think! Critical thought and analysis is half the battle, the other half is having the guts to go for it.

Shop around for the lowest APR - When most people find a property, they rush off to their local bank for a mortgage loan. I don't. I rush off to my nearest computer. I'm part of a very connected household so I normally don't have to go far. There are computers all over the place. I even carry a portable device with me so I have internet access on the go. After grabbing my computer, I go to my favorite website to compare mortgages - Bankrate.com. This makes me different from most investors, even the seasoned ones. I shop for my mortgages nationally. National lenders offer much better interest rates than local lenders. National lenders have deep pockets and streamlined staff, automation systems and services. Local lenders simply can't compete and their interest rates show it. In business, every little bit helps give your company a competitive edge and real estate is no different. A few percentage points could mean thousands or tens of thousands of dollars saved over the life of a mortgage loan. The thousands saved could translate into more properties for you!

Demand responsiveness from your real estate agent - The real estate business is all about speed! It's about getting a property under contract before the other guy. Unless you have a real estate license, you'll need an agent. Now, having said that, should you get a license? It depends. At the present time, I don't have a commercial real estate license. I'm not legal to buy and sale real estate for other people. At this time, I don't want a license. Why? I have an incredible real estate broker who is a proven real estate investor with over 30 properties. He is a straight shooter who has saved me hundreds of thousands of dollars by talking me out of bad deals. He really has my best interest at heart and he's worth every cent of his commission. Some of you may not be so lucky to have a connection like that. If that is the case, a real estate license can't hurt. The license doesn't take long to get and you can save on your commission while working some deals for other people to earn extra income. If you don't have a real estate agent, you need to find and hire a really good one. The agent needs to understand they work for you not the other way around. The agent should be competent and trustworthy. Over time, you will be able to see the agent's true intentions. You'll know if they are working to just close a deal or for your best interest. If they try to use high pressure tactics on you or if they are too slow carrying your offers, you need to fire them and get another agent. You need a good team surrounding you to succeed in this business.

Move quickly when opportunity surfaces - The business of real estate investing is filled with obstacles. Perhaps, the biggest obstacle is yourself. We have a natural tendency to avoid financial risks. This quality is the greatest hindrance to our personal success. It is the "play it safe" attitude that keeps us from reaching our full potential. You need to move quickly to lock up a good deal but your inner voice will say "No. We have time." The truth is you don't. You are competing with real estate investors worldwide and the seasoned ones aren't gun shy. They see a good deal and they go for it. You have to train yourself to do that too. A door doesn't stay open forever. If you find an incredible deal and you've done your research and worked your math, go for it! Lock it up with a contract! Yes, there is risk involved but so what! The truth is we all leave this world penniless so what are you really risking anyway! When you avoid risk, you ensure one thing. You ensure you will never, ever reach for full potential.

I never get home inspection - I think home inspections are worthless. You pay a guy $300 to walk around your home, look for cracks in the walls, turn on/off water faucets and flip electrical switches and send you their findings on a fancy report. Home inspectors are quick to point out, their assessment is a detailed review of the the home in its present state. It tells you nothing about the lifespan of major systems in your home. When I first started out, I used a home inspector. Now I do my own assessments. I flip my own light switches. I turn on my own water faucets. I look for foundation problems all by myself. Once, I paid for a home inspection and the inspector failed to inform me I had galvanized steel water pipes in my crawl space. Galvanized steel water pipes were used in the 60s. The problem with these pipes is...well...they are made out of steel. Steel corrodes over time when it exposed to water. If these water pipes go undetected, eventually they will burst! My pipes burst and caused extensive water damage. What is the home inspectors liability in all this? Nothing. The legal language of the home inspection contract protects them from these types of events. In my case, all I needed to know was galvanized steel pipes corrode and have a limited lifespan. If I would have known that, I would have had those pipes promptly replaced and protected myself from a massive headache. I'll never use a home inspector again. Anything can be fixed and I purchase my properties so far under market value that if I miss anything, I'll be ok.

Always view the property in person - I've learned of a growing trend of real estate investors buying properties solely off the internet. These investors flip through a few photos and then dish out hundreds of thousands of dollars without actually seeing their purchase with their own eyes. I find this unbelieveable. Listing agents aren't buffoons. They are very skilled at their profession. Through experience agents become very adept at presenting a home for sale. Every home has its high points and flaws. Agents focus on the characteristics that make a home more desirable and avoid presenting the flaws. If you have a home with mold in it, do you really think the agent will post a picture of the mold on the Multi-Listing Service? Of course not. Yes, the agent will disclose the mold for sure but you won't see a picture of it on the listing. Listing agents are professional sellers. Don't ever forget that. Ultimately, there is no one across this world who will look out for your best interest more than you. You need to see a property for yourself. You need to get a first hand view of the floorplan. Is the kitchen open or closed off to the living room? Where are the cable jacks? Does the placement of the television compliment the room or make it less functional? Is there adequate storage? What is the condition of the walls, carpet, HVAC system, plumbing and electrical? These are some difficult questions to answer simply by looking at four pictures from an internet listing. If you buy properties strictly off the internet, you are accepting incredible risk. Make sure you are the right kind of person that can accept that risk and still sleep at night.

Never, ever rent to family - There are all kinds of problems with renting to family. Let me count the ways. First, unless you rent your dwelling to family at market value, you are ineligible for most federal tax deductions. A dwelling that is rented to a family member below market rate is considered a personal use home not a real estate business. It's like owning a second home. At the time of this writing, you can still deduct mortgage interest but the deductions are not as powerful as owning your own real estate business. By owing a business, you can deduct mileage, local and state taxes, lodging, repairs and more. Everyone should consult a tax attorney or advisor for specifics because only a few people have the right business structure to report their holdings on a Schedule C. Most investors will need to report their real estate holdings on a Schedule E. Right now, everyone needs to remember this, never rent to family! In most cases, you'll likely rent it below market rate because you'll want to help them out. For a time your family members may pay faithfully. However, I would expect to see minor violations of the lease agreement over time. The family member may start to pay late. At other times they may not pay at all. What are you going to do? Evict a family member? No. In most cases you'll just deal with it robbing yourself of your future wealth in the process.

If you want to be rich, use a real estate agent and management company - What is your goal? If you really want to be rich, you'll need to control a lot of properties. If you ever hope to reach your goal, you will need to define your role. You only have so much time in a day. Managing a property takes time, energy and effort. Finding deals takes time, energy and effort. And finding financing takes time, energy and effort. What do you want your role to be? When I first started, I felt managing my own properties was the way to go. I figured I'd save 10% right from the start and I'll use that extra savings to buy more properties. Managing your own properties for a small investor is ok but impractical for a large one. In my case, I have a lot of properties and my real estate portfolio is growing as we speak. It is not easy to chase down so many tenants to collect rent, coordinate maintenance and service calls and so on. I've defined my role in my company. I have three jobs I am responsible for:

- I find new real estate deals.
- I secure financing.
- I oversee the rehab.

That's it. I have plenty of time in any given day to do my part. Outsourcing and independent contractors handle everything else to keep my business running smoothly. With an organizational structure like this, I'm able to grow as large as I want to.

Only buy real estate in cities with explosive population growth - If you are a buy and hold investor like me, you are in it for the long haul. Additionally, you'll need your properties to produce income. In short, you'll need tenants and lots of them. Follow census trends for the city or cities you plan to operate in. Focus on those cities growing fast and avoid cities where the population is decreasing. A nice home or apartment building doesn't do you any good if you have no tenants to rent to.

Only buy real estate in cities with growing economies - A city loaded with people does you no good if they are all unemployed. You need working tenants so they will have money to pay you rent. Call me a master of the obvious but it may surprise you how many people miss this vital fact. These investors make bonehead moves like buying an investment property in a city losing people and jobs fast! Areas like these are a stone's throw from becoming the set for the next zombie apocalypse movie with vacant, empty wastelands of junk homes, apartment and buildings.

Chapter 11

"Success is stumbling from failure to failure with no loss of enthusiasm."

- Winston S. Churchill

Final thoughts

I couldn't have picked a more fitting quote to describe my life. I purchased bad stocks, securities, real estate and bonds. I've started companies that failed. I've lost thousands on some deals but I've made thousands more on others. Don't misunderstand me, there is considerable risk in real estate. There is considerable risk in everything but if you keep trying, the odds are you'll succeed. My first two books never made the bestseller list. There is a good chance this one may not either but I keep trying! I keep going for it! And you should too! Life gives us nothing. It's up to us to go out and earn what we think we deserve. Failure is not an easy pill to swallow. It is quite bitter. People may laugh at you but remember, the Greeks laughed at Pythagoras when he first theorized the world was round almost 2000 years before Columbus was even born! If I can leave you with a final thought, it is this. Go for it! The truth is you are running out of time. A human's lifespan is short and the only way to reach your full potential is to go for it hard from the start.

If you enjoyed this book, please review it. Nothing is more precious to a writer than a review. It lets them know their countless hours spent researching and writing their book helped someone. There is no greater gift you can give a writer. There is no greater gift you can give me. This book was never written for money. I'm retired from the workforce at 41 years old. I'm a full-time investor. Writing this book was completely about capturing my trials, tribulations and experiences moving through the crazy world of real estate investing.

Somewhere in the world, there is a kid living in poverty like I was. Somewhere in this world, there is a kid wanting a better life. Somewhere there is a kid out there, hoping and praying for a better life. I hope my books find that kid because I was that kid once and I could have used the knowledge, wisdom and experience instead of figuring things out for myself.

I wish you all good luck and if you come across my previous two books **"Get Rich Off A Minimum Wage Income and 179 Days! The Story of a Combat Weatherman in Afghanistan"**, please read them and write me a review. And applaud me because I'm still trying for that bestseller. Persistent is the key to success in everything. Godspeed to you all. - Kevin McNeely

THE END